38 34
RA RG
MARCH 9 72
U. S. PENITENTIARY

Cast

ated

MY
EIGHT
MONTHS
IN
PRISON

Castrated

MY EIGHT MONTHS IN PRISON

BY RALPH GINZBURG

DESIGNED BY HERB LUBALIN

 For additional information, write to publisher. To order additional copies, see your bookseller or send $2.95 (plus 30¢ for postage and handling) to: Avant-Garde Books, 110 W. 40th St., New York, N.Y. 10018. International Standard Book Number: 0-913568-00-7. Library of Congress catalog number: 72-96906. Trademark "Avant-Garde" is registered at the U.S. Patent Office, Washington, D.C.

For Shoshana, who holds me
captive without irons or chains

On the morning of February 17, 1972, when Ralph Ginzburg was taken into custody, The Committee for a Free Press—an ad hoc group of distinguished artists, writers, editors, publishers and lawyers—took a full-page ad in *The New York Times* to express outrage over Ralph Ginzburg's imprisonment. The following are statements from that ad.

"The criminality in Ralph's case is on the part of those sending him to jail."—Melvin M. Belli, attorney.

"This decision by the Supreme Court is so primitive as to be breathtaking. Our baneful Puritan inheritance is nowhere more evident than in the *Ginzburg* case. That the Supreme Court of the United States, in all its majesty, could come to such a petty decision is hardly believable."—James Jones, novelist.

"The conviction of Ralph Ginzburg is one of the great crimes of the century."—Melvin L. Wulf, Legal Director, American Civil Liberties Union.

"Just this week *The New York Times* devoted an entire page to marking the 50th anniversary of the publication of *Ulysses*, James Joyce's masterpiece. We all know of the vilification of that book when Random House attempted to publish it here in the United States. What a sad, tragic state of affairs that, after all these years, the courts have not learned the lessons of history."–Jerome Snyder, artist.

"The U.S. Government is trying to legislate taste. This is a clear threat to freedom of the press–the right of people to read what they wish, of publishers to publish."–Sloan Wilson, novelist.

"I am a humorist, but for the first time in my life I've found a situation where I just can't see anything funny. Ginzburg's jailing is a tragedy. All of us concerned with free expression must protest this cruel distortion of justice." –Dan Greenburg, author.

"I think the prison term is outrageous."–Nat Hentoff, journalist.

"I consider Mr. Ginzburg's conviction absurd and unjust, and believe it in the best interests of everyone if it were reversed. The way to go about cleaning up pruriency is not by prudery and punishment, but by education. Toward that end, *Eros* was itself something of a contribution–paradoxical as that may appear to some."–Ashley Montagu, anthropologist.

"The Supreme Court held Ralph Ginzburg guilty of violating a standard that it has applied to no one else. He did mildly what the same court allows others to do blatantly. This is an unforgivable injustice. The law is shamed." –Professor Alexander M. Bickel, Yale Law School.

"In retrospect, and in view of the dreadful stuff legally on sale today, *Eros* emerges as a genuinely beautiful publication, treating sex in a very aesthetic fashion. I consider it an anachronism and an outrage that Ralph Ginzburg should go to jail when the lowest kinds of appeals to sadism and perversion flood the newsstands unmolested."–I.F. Stone, columnist.

"The conviction and incarceration of Ralph Ginzburg recall the wisdom and warning of Justice Louis Brandeis. In 1928, he said, 'Experience should teach us to be most on our guard to protect liberty when the government's purposes are beneficient. The greatest dangers to liberty lurk in insidious encroachments by men of zeal, well-meaning but without understanding.' The sustaining of Mr. Ginzburg's conviction by the Supreme Court is an anachronism and a tragic abrogation of First Amendment freedoms. The true 'victim' in Mr. Ginzburg's case is, unfortunately, the Bill of Rights itself."—Hugh M. Hefner, Publisher, *Playboy*.

"The Ginzburg case represents a cruel injustice, a stupid exaggeration of the native streak of vindictive malevolence toward what gives pleasure. The irony is that Mr. Ginzburg has won his case in practice; that is, America has changed somewhat about pleasure, and he is being punished under a decrepit influence from the past."—Herbert Gold, novelist.

"An incredible and terrifying miscarriage of justice." —Barney Rosset and Fred Jordan, Grove Press.

"Publishers stand united behind the principle that freedom is no freedom at all if it is accorded only to the accepted and inoffensive. It is not only ironic, but unjust that a man is today being jailed for publishing ten years ago what is now regarded by most as inoffensive. This case should serve as a warning that there is no guarantee of freedom in a democratic society, that what can happen in a totalitarian society can happen here. We say that governmental interference in the free flow of ideas without a proven danger to society is not the proper function of government, and should be resisted by all who value freedom. To jail a man for *one day* for exercising this freedom is outrageous; to do so for three years is grotesque."—Kenneth D. McCormick, Chairman, Freedom to Read Committee, Association of American Publishers.

"The prison sentence for Ralph Ginzburg is almost unbelievable in this country. It's not only a violation of the Constitution's First Amendment, but a violation of everything decent and moral—yes, moral."—Harry Golden, author-editor.

"In my opinion, the First Amendment guarantees that right of any person to send literature of any kind to another person who is willing to receive it. Furthermore, Ralph Ginzburg was convicted under a rule of law never before announced but adopted by the Supreme Court for the first time in his case. Under the circumstances, I do not consider it constitutional or just to require Mr. Ginzburg to serve a prison sentence."—Professor Tom Emerson, Yale Law School.

"The jailing of Ralph Ginzburg is a tragic anachronism: movies, theaters and newsstands today are filled with erotica that make *Eros* seem quaint. The Supreme Court must not be blind to the state of society, which now allows total license in the arts. The Court must not mock all reason by sending Ralph Ginzburg to jail in a time when the Sensuous Woman is on the Johnny Carson Show."—Ralph Schoenstein, author.

"The Executive Committee of the American Society of Magazine Editors vigorously protests the imprisonment of Ralph Ginzburg as an exceedingly grave threat to freedom of the press and an undoubted violation of the First Amendment. We join our voices to all others urging that this senseless imprisonment be forthwith averted."—William B. Arthur (former Editor, *Look*), Anderson Ashburn (*American Machinist*), Patricia Carbine (*McCall's*), Sey Chassler (*Redbook*), Clay Felker (*New York*), Hubert P. Luckett (*Popular Science*), Geraldine Rhoads (*Woman's Day*), Ray Robinson (*Seventeen*), Ruth Whitney (*Glamour*).

"Mr. Ginzburg's conviction is a threat to freedom of the press. I am outraged that he is taking the rap for an affair that wouldn't even bring him into court in 1972."—Garth Hite, Publisher, *The Atlantic Monthly*.

"When I think of what is being exhibited on the stage, heard and seen in the cinema, and printed everywhere in every kind of medium, the charge against Ralph Ginzburg—and the vindictive prison sentence—is nothing less than outrageous. This serves no purpose, sets no example, is a personal persecution."—Louis Untermeyer, author-editor.

"Ralph Ginzburg's conviction and jailing strike me as being farcical, mind-boggling and outrageous."—Bruce Jay Friedman, author.

"After all the legal, moral and psychological arguments are done, the fact remains that a man is going to prison for publishing and advertising stuff a few years ago that today would hardly raise an eyebrow in your dentist's office. This is the folly, the menace of all censorship—it lays down rules for all time which are ludicrous a short time later. If it is right that Ralph Ginzburg go to jail, then in all justice the same court that sentenced him should proceed at once to close down ninety percent of the movies now playing and the newspapers that carry their advertising. Compared to the usual run of entertainment in this country, Ginzburg's publications and his ads are on a par with the *National Geographic*."—Arthur Miller, playwright.

The door to the cell slammed shut and there I was behind bars. The ten-year ordeal of courtroom histrionics, legalistic double-talk and dashed hopes had ended at last. I found myself in the tiny lockup of the Federal District Court at Lewisburg, Pennsylvania. The date was February 17, 1972.

Except for the fact that my wife Shoshana had needed smelling salts at the very last minute, everything had gone smoothly, all things considered. My kids had been prepared emotionally for the long separation, my office staff had been instructed on how to carry on without me, and my wife's material needs had been provided for.

As I sat alone in the claustrophobifacient cell, furnished with two fancy mahogany chairs and a toilet seat, my mind throbbed with questions: Had I made a mistake in abandoning my plan to chain myself to the Jefferson Memorial? (One of my lawyers had led me to believe that I would be released in a matter of weeks if only I would refrain from any show of defiance.) Should I have fled to Canada, as I had at one point made elaborate plans to do? Would the public be made aware of my imprisonment and the constitutional issues involved? Which prison would I be sent to and what would prison life be like?

My thoughts were soon interrupted by the appearance of the U.S. Marshal, a friendly, rotund man in his late fifties, named Cotner, who removed me from my cell and apologetically clamped me in manacles. We were joined by another marshal and another prisoner, a young black from Lewisburg Penitentiary who had been to court that morning to be resentenced for having murdered a fellow inmate over a carton of cigarettes. The four of us descended the steps of the courthouse to a waiting sedan. News photographers swarmed toward me. I tried to look appropriately grim, though, in truth, I was feeling nothing.

The sedan sped toward the outskirts of Lewisburg, and I wondered again which prison I would be taken to. My lawyers had told me that it would be either the maximum-security penitentiary at Lewisburg or the minimum-security prison camp at Allenwood.

The prisoner beside me in the back seat, I noticed, was wearing a bizarre combination: a navy pea jacket, green stocking cap, suntan pants and shirt, and brown high-top shoes that looked like something out of a Sears, Roebuck catalog, circa 1910. His outfit, I was soon to learn, was standard Federal prison garb, a confusion of armed forces surplus and items made by prisoners at various Federal institutions.

In our forced intimacy, I felt compelled to converse with my comrade-in-bondage and was amazed to find him an affable, polite, even gentle human being. From this impression, which was later reinforced by my dealings with scores of other inmates, I learned that you can't judge a crook by his cover. That is, the most dangerous criminal, capable of the most hideous deeds under certain circumstances, in everyday life looks and acts just like you or me.

At the Lewisburg city limits the marshal turned off the highway and onto an ominously beautiful, deserted, tree-lined drive. In the distance loomed a towering edifice surrounded by a high gray wall. It reminded me of Count Dracula's Castle. This, I soon realized, was Lewisburg Penitentiary. My mouth went dry.

When the marshal stopped the car in front of the main gate, I became even more apprehensive —until he opened the door and said, "Jackson, you come with me. Ginzburg, you stay here."

The drive to Allenwood, 18 miles away, took 25 minutes. We entered through an open, unguarded, grillwork gate and drove past fields covered with hoarfrost. We stopped at a cluster of low frame buildings that resembled a World War II army camp—which, in fact, Allenwood had been. The marshal led me into the small administration building in the center of the compound. I was immediately overwhelmed, and depressed, by the subway-rush-hour-like congestion and din. Inmates shouted to one another on long, slow-moving lines into the mess hall, commissary and offices of caseworkers; a loudspeaker blared unintelligible commands to the prison population at large; and a cacophony of transistor radios screamed against an obligato of clumping, mud-laden boots. This assault on my auditory senses, this hellish music, abetted by the stench of cigarette smoke and body odor, was to become the most constant, excruciating form of torture I would have to endure during my eight months in prison.

The marshal shepherded me into the office of the prison administrative officer, a Mr. Joseph Andracchio, where he removed my handcuffs and was given a "body receipt" for me. Mr. Andracchio enrolled my name and sentence on the prison records (setting me down for *five* years, instead of three, because of a court clerk's error) and christened me: "38124-134."

A guard escorted me to the prison clothing room, where I was "dressed in" with the same sort of outfit that the inmate in the sedan had been wearing, and to the barbershop, where an inmate performed the government's symbolic rite of cropping my hair and cutting off my mustache.

That night, I lay on my lumpy, narrow top bunk in the huge, impersonal dormitory known as The Jungle, surrounded by 150 snoring, grunting, farting men, and thought about the intimate, incense-laden hush of my bedroom at home. I longed for the warmth of my wife's body sleeping beside me and worried about her safety. Would she be molested by crank-callers, house-breakers–*suitors!*– in my absence? Could my children possibly survive this separation unscarred? Could I? How many more nights like this would I have to bear? It was a nightmare from which my only escape was sleep.

The next morning I was interviewed by the camp's assistant warden for a job assignment. Prior to my surrender, my wife and I had become so disillusioned over the outcome of the *Eros* case that we were seriously considering deserting the publishing world to take up a simple pastoral life in the wilds of Newfoundland. Here at Allenwood I saw a chance to pick up whatever farming skills might be necessary for our adventure and I requested work on the prison farm. "No soap," said the assistant warden. He consigned me instead to Mr. Andracchio as a busywork clerk. Nearly all other new inmates, I later discovered, were assigned to the farm automatically, since the older inmates considered farm work demeaning. But the Bureau of Prisons in Washington, I also later discovered, had been concerned that I might become an organizer and instigator of unrest at

Allenwood, and had wanted me assigned to headquarters where I could be kept under close scrutiny. (As it happened, on my very first day in prison I was contacted by a group of inmates who wanted me to help organize a protest. But I declined, since I had decided long in advance to be a model prisoner; my quarrel was not with the Bureau of Prisons but with the courts, our system of "justice.")

On the job, I worked in tandem with Martin Sweig—the ex-administrative assistant to Speaker of the House of Representatives John W. McCormack—who had been convicted of conspiracy, bribery and perjury in connection with misuse of his office. I found Marty to be a contemptible individual, a shameless sycophant of the prison brass, Uriah Heep incarnate. My work consisted of refiling years of misfiled index cards and catching Marty's errors. It was a crescendo of boredom. The only saving grace-notes I can remember were witnessing the parole of a double murderer who was serving life, glimpsing occasional beautiful moments of reunion in the adjacent visiting room, and peering into the confidential dossiers of some of the inmates, including those of several supposedly tough Mafiosi whose files were stamped "Pederast."

As days that seemed like weeks and weeks that seemed like months dragged by, I began to fall into the rhythm of prison life. I became "institutionalized," as prisoners say. No one who has not undergone this complete psychic castration can possibly understand its horror. Every last vestige of a man's individuality and independence is stripped from him:

- His name is replaced by a number—I responded to "38124-134" almost reflexively.

• He must eat whatever is put before him—Hot chili and greasy pork chops supplanted my wonted cottage cheese and soybeans.

• His clothes no longer express his identity—Inmates take desperate steps to deviate from the norm, and even I, who normally do not care much about my appearance, risked disciplinary action by having my wife, during a visit, embroider my number on my jacket (in purple, no less).

• He is forced to do meaningless work—I was reduced to filing cards in alphabetical order, where formerly I had striven to create magazines of international importance.

• He is allowed no private communication with the outside world—Every letter I sent or received was censored, though my wife and I managed to overcome this by using a celsitudinous vocabulary that went over the heads of our guards.

• He must obsequiously obey men he considers his inferiors—I was once forced to throw out my coveted copies of *The Sierra Club Bulletin* when a guard capriciously ordered me to do so.

• Finally, he is allowed no sexual outlet—I, like the other men, became a robot-like eunuch, and it was painfully clear to me that deprivation of manhood is really what prison is all about.

And so *malgré soi* I assumed the identity of 38124-134. Awaking by lifelong habit at 3 a.m., I lay passively on my bunk until the shrill electronic whistle sounded at 5:45 to awaken "the population." With the other prisoners, I shuffled into breakfast at 6, then cleaned the dormitory and toilets until Work Call at 7:30. The main midday meal—termed dinner because it was the heaviest of the day—was eaten at 10:15, an hour when people on "the street" were usually having their midmorning coffee. I returned to work till 3:45, when supper was served. In the leisure time after supper, until Lights Out at 10, while the rest of the prison gambled for cigarettes, slurped Tang, or watched shoot-'em-ups on TV (they were known as "training films"), I would sit alone on the back steps of the dormitory and look up at the bright, fixed stars, or go down to a specially-designated stretch of road in the middle of the compound and run back and forth like a rat in an exercise wheel until I was tired enough to sleep. If ever I forgot where I was, I was soon reminded by the piercing, unnerving whistle that periodically signaled Count Time when guards would check the inmates to be sure that no one had escaped. (Eight inmates did escape during the months I was at Allenwood. It is to the credit of the Bureau of Prisons that it continues to maintain the camp as a minimum-security installation, despite the high escape rate, rather than punish all 325 inmates for the transgressions of a few.)

Each day at Allenwood was just like the one before it and the only time I became the *real* Ralph Ginzburg was during visits. I had visits from friends, relatives, staff members, and, dearest of all to me, my wife. They were as adrenalin to a failing heart. I would prolong them in advance by starting to prepare 24 hours early: shining my shoes, ironing my clothes, trimming my nails, and making extensive notes so that I couldn't possibly fail to bring up all the subjects about which I had been yearning for news.

My wife came once a week, usually on Fridays, bringing the children with her every fourth visit. Starting a half hour too early, I would peer out the dormitory window for a glimpse of our big old station wagon raising dust along the road. Invariably, it rolled into the gravel parking lot outside the visiting room at five minutes to eight, and

"38124-134" would be summoned over the loudspeaker. As my wife filled out the required visitor's form, a guard would shake me down and then admit me to the visiting room. My wife and I would shyly and hungrily take hands, search each other for signs of change and make a bee-line for the most secluded table, farthest from the guards and other visitors.

Ritualistically, my wife would take out a small brown notebook and go over all points of business, legal and household affairs that required decisions by me. Carefully she would make note of my instructions, to act upon them the following week. This usually took until noon, when it was time for the prisoners and visitors in the visiting room to dine in the mess hall, on standard prison fare (cost to visitors: 70¢). After the other inmates and their visitors had left the mess hall, my wife and I would linger as long as possible to enjoy the view of the countryside that the room afforded and its relative privacy—no guards were present.

After lunch, with pressing matters aside, we would really begin to relax and enjoy each other's company. I would regale my wife with anecdotes concerning the characters and incidents of prison life. I told her about my conversations with celebrities such as Bobby Baker, Carmine De Sapio, Gen. Carl Turner, Clifford Irving and Guy Gillette, the dauntless war resister. I would present her with cameos of such unforgettable personalities as the Treasury Department engraver who was at Allenwood for having done a little moonlighting on the side; the mayor of a small Western Pennsylvania town who was in prison on a conspiracy charge, along with his chief of police and the town's bookie; the "hired gun" who offered me his services if and when I ever needed them after we both got out; the hail-fellow-well-met who was the confidant of many of the prison's most notorious inmates and who allegedly had been jailed for bank embezzlement but who, as I knew from my work in the office, was actually a former assistant regional director of the FBI. And I fascinated her with descriptions of the life of the only inmate with whom I ever shared confidences, a convicted counterfeiter, drug-pusher, gigolo, car thief, mugger—and really sweet guy—named Lefty. My wife, in turn, would fill me in on the blossoming of our children, convey the messages of well-wishers and describe the changes taking place in New York City. Never did we discuss the real thing on our mind: our mutual suffering and the anguish of separation.

At 3:15, *sharp*, a guard would advance menacingly to advise us that visiting hours were over. We would walk to the edge of the parking lot and I would stand there alone in the frosty air as my wife backed up the car and left the compound, pausing for a last glimpse of me and, in symbolic gesture, to toss me her heart. I would walk back through the visiting room, be re-frisked by a guard, and, to preserve my sanity, willfully lapse again into the role of 38124-134.

The Bureau of Prisons is the most smoothly run department of the Federal government I have ever encountered, and its most efficient instrument—insidiously so—is parole. The promise of parole is used to keep inmates on their best behavior; in effect, a man's own desire for freedom is used to enslave him. *No* topic—not sex, not politics, not religion, not wealth—is more constantly or agonizingly discussed than parole. No letter is written, no conversation is struck up, no opinion is expressed, no grimace is made to a guard, no argument is begun, no button is sewed on without concern for its possible effect upon parole. And no prisoner was ever more obsessed with the subject of parole than I.

Because of a special section of the law under which I had been sentenced, it was possible, theoretically, for me to be paroled on the very first day I was imprisoned. But, as I later learned in prison, this provision of the law, although intended otherwise by Congress, is used chiefly by judges to get importuning lawyers and defendants off their backs and shift to the parole board the burden of authorizing early release. Never in the history of the U.S. Board of Parole has a prisoner actually been liberated immediately after incarceration. Nevertheless, I began to work, and hope, for an early parole as soon as I was imprisoned. I filed a parole application and had business associates, friends, relatives, libertarian organizations, judges I knew, distinguished artists and writers, and fellow members of the West Side YMCA in New York send letters supporting my application to the parole board. This was all exceedingly difficult to accomplish from prison, considering the limited facilities and restrictions on correspondence. (Try checking an address in the Bronx from Allenwood, Pa., without the use of a phone or directory). But my early efforts were to no avail. On April 27th, the United States Board of Parole denied my petition. I reapplied a month later and again was turned down. This second denial flung me into a frenzy of despair. "I've *got* to get out of here!" kept running through my head like a chant.

Deliverance was to come through the ardent efforts of my wife, for whom ministering to my needs is a religion. Seeing me in my tortured state drove her to brazen action. She climbed on the backs of our lawyers, the prison psychiatrist, the chief administrative officer of the parole board and (indirectly) even the judge who had sentenced me, and spurred them with the idea that I was about to commit suicide, that I had made plans to hang myself from the prison flagpole, and that they would carry the guilt for my death through history if they did not act *immediately*.

Under her onslaught, our lawyers convinced the judge who convinced the parole board to schedule a special hearing on my release on July 27th, overruling its own earlier decision not even to reconsider the possibility of my parole until November.

On the day of the hearing, my wife flew to Washington and appeared before all eight members of the board at its chambers in the Home Owners' Loan Corporation Building on Indiana Avenue. She was dressed and coifed as a paradigm of respectability, in contrast to her usual avant-garde costume. Reviving her most cultivated Sarah Lawrence inflection, she explained that I was not a money-grubbing pornographer, as some people had supposed, but a publisher of lofty journalistic and artistic purpose. She invoked for them the suffering of the many members of my family bereft by my absence: my blind sister; widowed mother; diabetic, 11-year-old mulatto nephew and his older schizophrenic brother—to say nothing of our three children and herself. Trembling with emotion, she pointed out the supreme irony of my being locked away for publishing an extraordinary magazine like *Eros* at a time when into the prisons of the United States, including Allenwood, through the agency of the United States Mail and with the sanction of duly appointed prison authorities, the most sordid and crude of sexpapers were freely circulated. Finally, in the tradition of women through the ages who have appeared before tribunals of justice to plead for the freedom of their lovers, she entreated them to release me. The tears in her eyes were matched by those welling in the eyes of several of the casehardened members of the board, and she knew then that I had won my parole.

Late that afternoon, Franklin Walker, chief

caseworker at Allenwood Prison, summoned me to his office and gave me the news that my parole had been granted, effective October 10th. I received the news with mixed feelings; I was elated to have the end in sight, but bitter over the long 10 weeks' delay. Normally, parole is followed by liberation in a week or 10 days. Apparently the decision to let me go had been reached by compromise.

The manner in which a prisoner serves time is described by convicts as either "hard" or "easy." Once I had made parole, my time became easy. I requested a change of job, to one that would take me out of doors into the beautiful midsummer weather. My request was granted and I was appointed groundskeeper and sexton of the prison church (the Jewish inmates, who are disproportionately numerous at Allenwood, were aghast; *"A shonde un a kharpe!"*). Also, I began an ambitious regimen of self-improvement. I reverently studied the biographies of Freud, Lincoln and Bach. I tried to learn to play the church organ. I taught myself to identify many wildflowers and constellations. And I began jogging and weightlifting for two hours a day. (I ended up by losing 30 pounds.)

When a prisoner has been given a release date, provided he will have served at least six months, he is permitted a three-day furlough, ostensibly to help him readjust to society, line up a job or, as in my case, rescue an ailing business.

On August 16th, my furlough began. My wife, with the station wagon freshly washed, picked me up and we drove to a prearranged meeting with my editorial staff at the Georgia-Pacific paper mill in upstate New York which supplies paper for *Moneysworth*. There we conducted a marathon workfest, resolving problems, renewing bonds of colleagueship and exuberantly laying plans for the future.

When the meeting was over, my wife and I departed for a serendipitous shunpike tour of the Adirondacks and Finger Lakes region, inspecting vineyards, watching a polo match, climbing Buttermilk Falls, reveling in the graciousness of pre-Revolutionary Lincklaen Inn at Cazenovia, gorging ourselves on green apples, unabashedly crying over the joys and travail of characters in "Fiddler on the Roof," sharing a glass of Lancers wine at midnight supper, and even tramping for a while in the fragrance of the Northville-Lake Placid Trail. It was a phantasmagoric tapestry of rapture-interwoven-with-rapture that we will be able to look back on for the rest of our lives.

Although, as I have indicated, the furlough was a sublime experience overall, its summital moment came right at the outset. During the half year of my imprisonment I had felt no sexual desire whatsoever, and I had become anxious over my potency. Would I be able to rise to The Occasion? As my wife drove into the prison, my heart was pounding as much with apprehension as with expectation. After she had signed me out, she told me that she hadn't yet checked out of her motel because she wanted to show me the place where she had so often stayed. We got into the car, I took the wheel, and we swung out onto the road toward the Sheraton Motor Inn at South Williamsport. As we began to commune in our heady new freedom, I tentatively allowed my hand to drop and touch my wife in a way that had been forbidden us these long months, and I was relieved to discover that mine was still the Power and the Glory (in fact, it threatened to tear my prison-issue trousers).

I must have made the 14 miles to the motel in record time. Still on the pretext of sight-seeing, my wife led me through the motel and to her room, unlocked the door, and began to rush around nervously and chatter about the view, the travel pamphlets on the dresser, and the sauna feature of the shower. I grabbed her by the wrist, drew her to me, and silenced her with a primordial kiss. The room, the view, time, and all other earthly concerns fell away from us. Wordlessly, we undressed. As my wife stood before me, reflected in the wall-length mirror behind her, I was overwhelmed by the lush revelation of things about her that are precious to me: a certain look in her eye, the conformation of her hands, the smell of her hair, the curve of her hip. It was a rich, slow-motion montage of delicious, lust-provoking images. Lost to all reason and restraint, we made love. The force of our orgasm shattered the damming walls of anxiety, doubt and repression that had built up during our enforced separation, and at the moment when the tidal wave of my wife's sexual passion burst through, all her other passions flooded close behind. Sobbing uncontrollably into my chest, Shoshana wept for all her loneliness, misery and pain—and for the joy of our reunion. I knew that I had freed her—and for the first time in five months, three weeks, and six days, I felt like a man.

At the end of the furlough, I returned to Allenwood, but I never really returned to prison. The weeks that followed were spent in fruitful preparation for my re-entry into society. Because my children were still out of school on vacation, my wife was able to make more frequent visits. We would sit for hours on a double-bench out on the grass in front of the visiting room. During these late-summer idylls, we got the inspiration for, and even managed to lay out the details of, two nonpareil new magazines that we hope to launch some day. Our immediate plans, however, were to restore *Moneysworth* to the level of editorial excellence and circulation it had reached before my imprisonment, and to revive *Avant-Garde*, which had fallen as an indirect victim of the government's barrage against *Eros*.

On my last morning at Allenwood, I shed my

prison uniform for a set of conservative "dress-outs" and bade farewell to my friends among the inmates and guards. There were as many good guys (like witty Mr. Campbell, charitable Mr. Streck and mustachioed Mr. Hoffman) and villains (like race-concious Mr. Kozari, rigid Mr. Whiting and sadistic Mr. Tubbs) among the guards as there were, relatively, among the inmates, and probably as there are in the world at large.

My wife and my daughter Lark picked me up and drove me to the prison gate, where I stepped out into the glare of TV cameras and a field of microphones and made the following statement:

In Contempt of the Supreme Court

I, Ralph Ginzburg, paroled prisoner, U.S. Bureau of Prisons convict number 38124-134, do hereby accuse the United States Supreme Court of high crimes and treason, namely, of mocking the Constitution, trammeling Freedom of the Press, and playing fast and loose with one man's liberty —mine.

I have just completed eight months in prison. I now face an additional four years and four months of probation and parole. I have been fined a Draconian $42,000. For a decade I have been dragged in and out of courtrooms, compelled to defend myself before the bar. In money, my defense has cost nearly a quarter of a million dollars. In emotional expenditure, the cost has been incalculable. My work has been defiled. My publications have been suppressed. My family has been tormented. My reputation has been besmirched. My career as a writer and publisher has all but been destroyed.

For what? What is the hideous crime for which

I have been so mercilessly flogged and declared an enemy of the people? I'll tell you what: I tried to give America its first beautiful, intellectual, emotionally mature, completely forthright magazine dealing with love and sex. Its name was *Eros*. Myriad awards for literary and artistic excellence were bestowed upon *Eros*, but when the Supreme Court gazed upon the magazine all it could see was "smut." It branded *Eros* "obscene" and banished me to prison. Let history mark that in the year Nineteen Hundred and Seventy-Two, in this supposedly civilized, professedly free society, a man was manacled and muzzled for trying to tell the truth about sex.

Normally, when a man has lived through an ordeal as I have, his inclination would be to go home and try to forget about the whole thing. After all, the prison gate is now behind me. But I have fought this case as a matter of principle right from the start, and I do not intend to give up now. It is my intention, as soon as I return to New York, to meet with my lawyers and representatives of the American Civil Liberties Union, Committee for a Free Press, Authors League, Association of American Publishers, American Library Association and other libertarian organizations that have supported me from the start, and lay plans for reopening my case. I *will* be vindicated. I don't care if it takes the rest of my life. I will carry the case back to the Supreme Court, for a third time, if necessary. I will not bear the stigma of guilt. I will never ever say "Uncle....Sam."

The reaction of the courts to my new appeal will give the American people a clear indication of the measure of justice they can expect from their courts. In a sense, in my new appeal, justice itself will be on trial. If the courts refuse to hear my

plea, if they deem my case a dead issue, they will thereby be telling the American people that the Constitution itself is a dead letter, and that individual liberty no longer exists. The American people will see, once and for all, whether justice in this country is a beautiful blindfolded woman or a deaf blind old man.

Having made my statement, I got into the car with my wife and daughter and began the 200-mile journey back to New York.